Who Am I?

Dee White

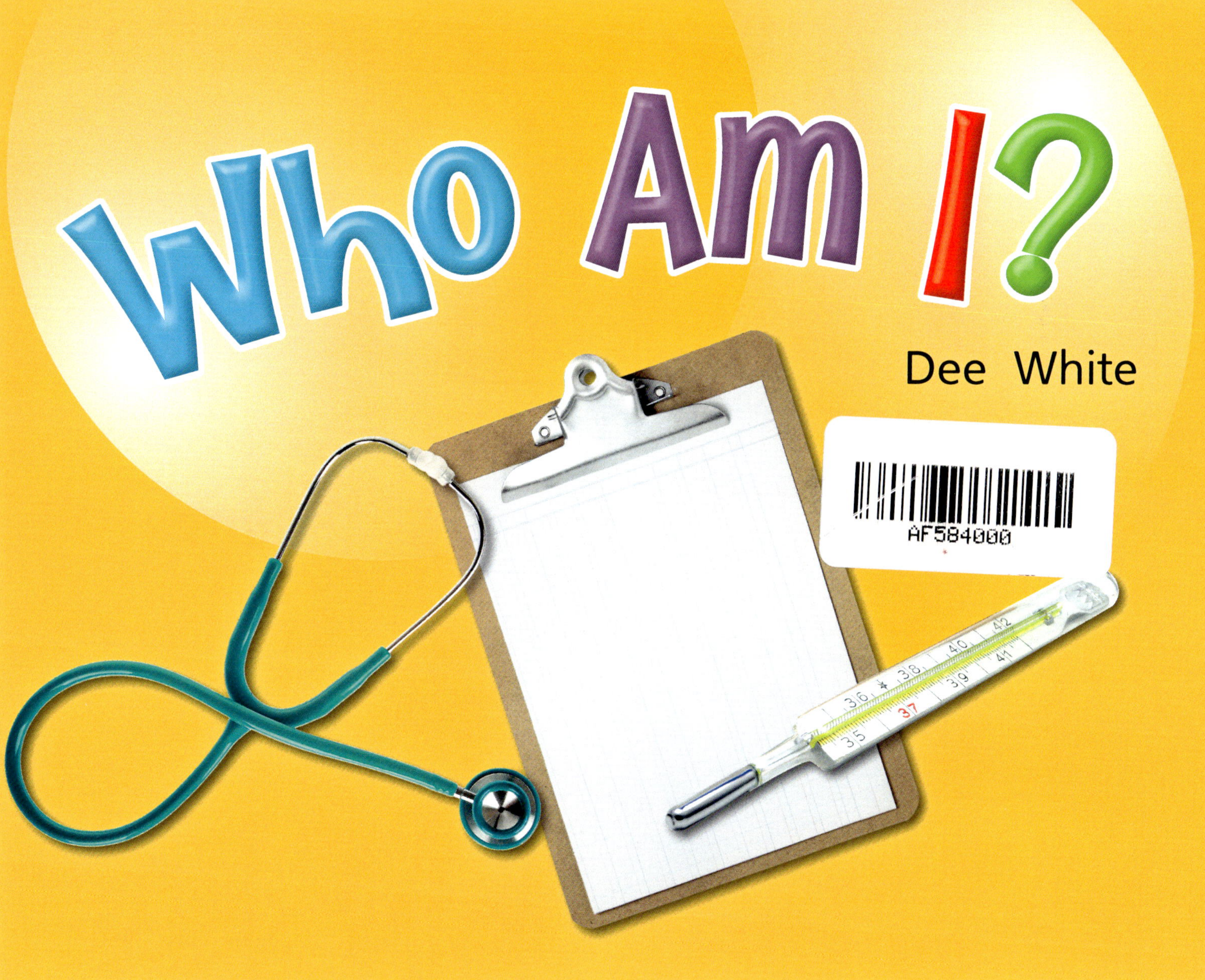

I like to dress up.
My friends like to dress up, too.
Can you guess who we are?

This is my stethoscope.

This is my clipboard.

I have a thermometer.

I am a doctor.

I help people get better when they are sick.

This is my hard hat.

This is my whistle.

I have a hose.

Who am I?

I am a firefighter.

I put out fires and save people's lives.

This is me!

This is my wig.

This is my red nose.

I have colourful clothes.

I am a circus clown.

I do funny things to make people laugh.

This is my hat.

This is my white coat.

I have a wooden spoon.

I am a chef.

I cook yummy food for people to eat.

This is my hat.

These are my overalls.

I have a brush.

I am a painter.

I help people to paint their houses.

This is my black hat.

This is my magic wand.

I have a pack of cards.

Who am I?

I am a magician.

I do lots of magic tricks.

This is me!

It is fun to dress up!
Who do you like to dress up as?

Index